A *fashionable* HISTORY *of the* SHOE

A FASHIONABLE HISTORY OF THE SHOE
was produced by

David West ⚲ Children's Books
7 Princeton Court
55 Felsham Road
London SW15 1AZ

This edition first published in the United States in
2003 by Raintree, a division of Reed Elsevier, Inc.,
Chicago, Illinois.

For information address the publisher:
Raintree
100 N. LaSalle
Suite 1200
Chicago, IL 60602

Author: Helen Reynolds
Editors: Jackie Gaff, Marta Segal Block
Picture Research: Carlotta Cooper
Designer: Julie Joubinaux

Library of Congress Cataloging-in-Publication Data:
Reynolds, Helen, 1956-
  The shoe / Helen Reynolds.
     v. cm. -- (Fashionable history of costume)
Summary: From foot bag to fashion fads -- Material matters --
Shape
shifting -- Sole survivors -- Walking tall -- Coming to heel -- The ties
that bind -- Slip on a sandal -- Sporting chances -- Shoes as art --
Men
in boots -- Women's boots -- Shoe technology.
Includes bibliographical references and index.
  ISBN 1-4109-0027-4 (lib. bdg.)
  1. Shoes--Juvenile literature. 2. Footwear--Juvenile literature. [1.
Shoes--History.] I. Title. II. Series.
  GT2130 .R49 2003
  391.4'13--dc21
                              2002153949

ISBN 1-4109-0027-4

07 06 05 04 03
10 9 8 7 6 5 4 3 2 1

PHOTO CREDITS:

Abbreviations: t-top, m-middle, b-bottom, r-right,
l-left, c-center.

The publisher would like to thank the following
for permission to reproduce photographs:
Front cover m – National Trust Photographic
Library/Roy Fox; front cover r – Rex Features
Ltd.; pages 3 & 22bl, 4br, 5br, 9tl, 10b, 11tr, 12
all, 12-13, 13 both, 15br, 17mr, 18tr, 19mr, 23t &
br, 25tr & br, 2bl & br, 26-27, 27tr & br – Rex
Features Ltd.; pages 4tr, 6br, 8tl, 10tl & tr, 16tr,
18tl - © Museum of London; page 6tr – University
of Missouri; page 6mr – University of Oregon
Museum of Natural History; pages 6bl, 14tl, 16bl,
17tr – Dover Books; pages 6-7, 9bl, 11bl, 14tr &
bl, 15tl, 16br, 26tr, 28l – Northampton Museums
and Art Gallery; pages 7t, 9tr – Hulton Archive;
page 8br – Board of Trustees of the National
Museums and Galleries on Merseyside (Walker Art
Gallery); pages 15tr, 18br, 20tr, 24bl, 24-25t –
Mary Evans Picture Library; page 20bl – Karen
Augusta, www.antique-fashion.com; page 20br –
Digital Stock; pages 21 all, 24-25b – Corbis
Images; page 22tl – 1969-282-55 Schiaparelli,
Elsa/Boots, c.1938/Philadelphia Museum of Art:
Gift of Mme Elsa Schiaparelli; pages 22-23 –
Irving Solero/The Museum at the Fashion Institute
of Technology; page 29t – Clarks.

Printed and bound in China

A *fashionable* HISTORY *of the* SHOE

Contents

SLIPPER SHOE

This soft leather shoe was the basic style of footwear worn by Europeans throughout the Middle Ages. It was made by sewing the upper to the sole, then turning it inside out—hence its name, the turnshoe.

SHOEMAKER'S CRAFT

Footwear was made by hand until shoemaking machines were invented in the 19th century.

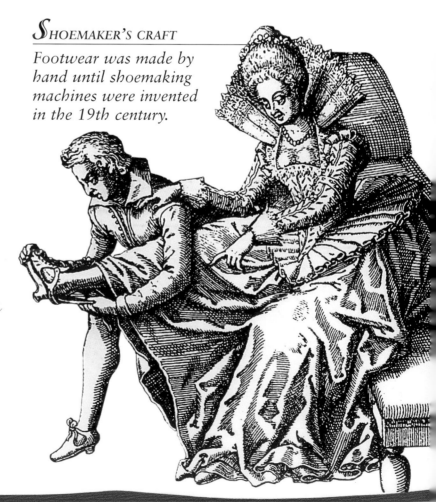

From Foot Bag to Fashion Fads

Shoes were invented to protect feet from rough ground and sharp objects, as well as to keep them warm in cold weather. They date back to prehistoric times, when people made baglike foot coverings out of furry animal skins, or simply wound leather strips around their feet and ankles. Over time, the basic design gradually improved until shoes had a base called a sole and a top part called an upper. Different types of shoes were introduced, from sturdy hobnailed boots for soldiers to fragile satin slippers for court ladies. Fashions came and went, and, just like today, some styles were sensible, others outrageously impractical.

HIGH FASHION

Standing would be tricky in this contemporary stiletto-heeled shoe, let alone walking. Its high heel is made possible by a sturdy steel core.

CHIC SHAPE

Originally designed for sports, the sneaker is now a fashionable everyday style.

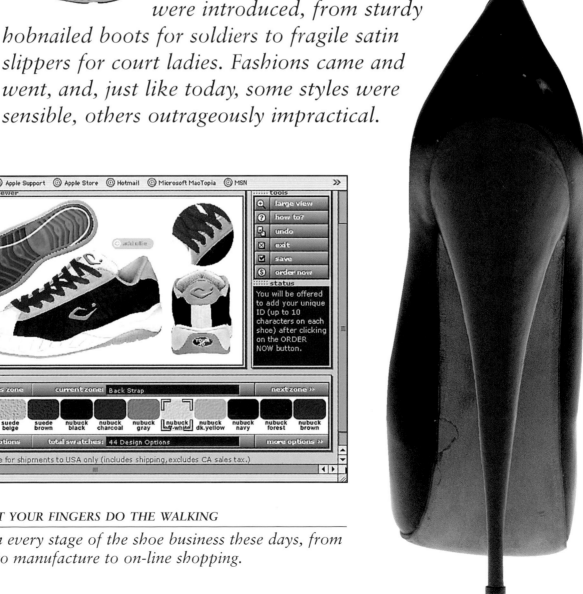

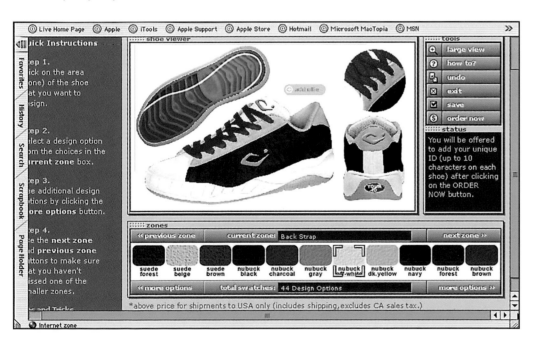

LET YOUR FINGERS DO THE WALKING

Computers are used in every stage of the shoe business these days, from design to manufacture to on-line shopping.

Material Matters

Around the world, early civilizations made shoes from the materials available to them, in styles suited to their local landscape and climate. The earliest known ancient Egyptian shoes, for example, were woven from papyrus reeds. These simple sandals let cool air circulate around the feet while protecting them from hot desert sands.

Looking at leather

Northern Europe's cold weather and rough ground meant that people needed more durable materials such as leather. The process of turning animal skins into leather is called tanning, and it has been practiced for more than 3,000 years. The thickest leathers were made by tanning cattle hides, while softer leathers were made from the skins of deer, goats, pigs, and sheep, or by splitting thick hides into thinner layers.

First footwear

These Native American shoes are among the oldest ever found. This shoe, left, was woven from plant fibers 9,000 years ago. The one above was made from leather and lined with grass around 1,000 years ago.

Clever clogs

The clog is a shoe carved from a single piece of wood. An extremely durable material, wood has been used in shoemaking for thousands of years.

6

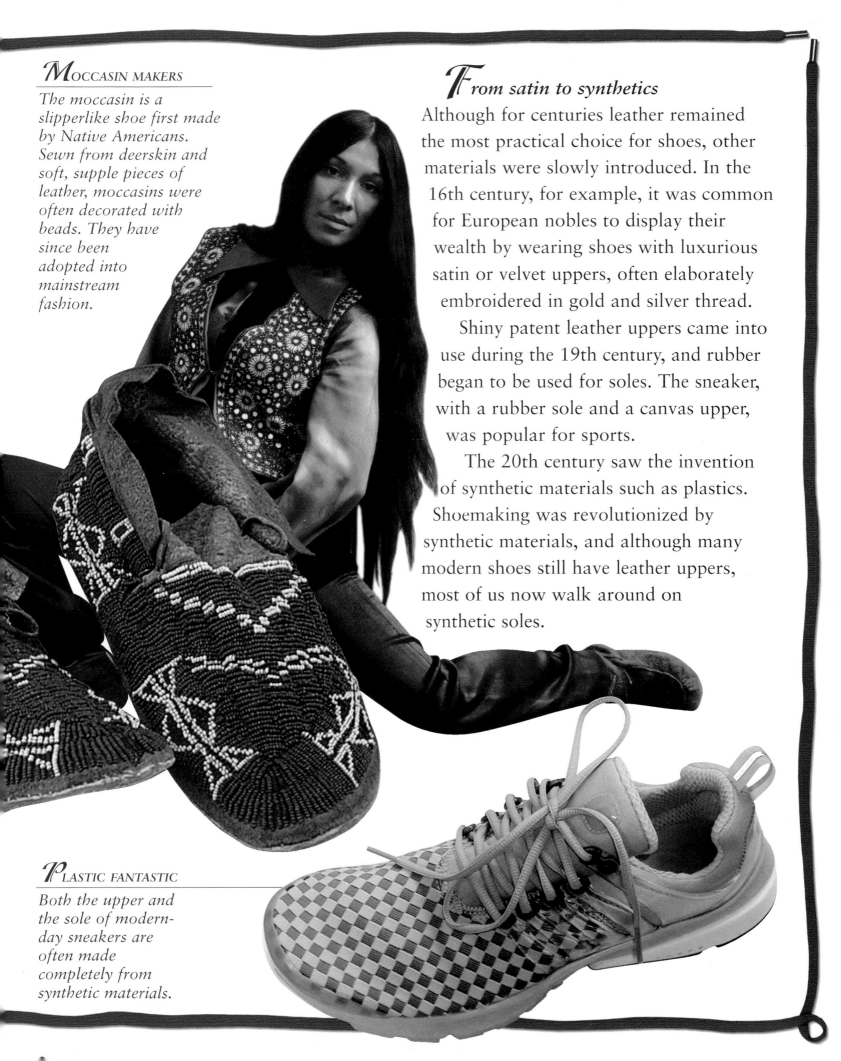

Moccasin makers

The moccasin is a slipperlike shoe first made by Native Americans. Sewn from deerskin and soft, supple pieces of leather, moccasins were often decorated with beads. They have since been adopted into mainstream fashion.

From satin to synthetics

Although for centuries leather remained the most practical choice for shoes, other materials were slowly introduced. In the 16th century, for example, it was common for European nobles to display their wealth by wearing shoes with luxurious satin or velvet uppers, often elaborately embroidered in gold and silver thread.

Shiny patent leather uppers came into use during the 19th century, and rubber began to be used for soles. The sneaker, with a rubber sole and a canvas upper, was popular for sports.

The 20th century saw the invention of synthetic materials such as plastics. Shoemaking was revolutionized by synthetic materials, and although many modern shoes still have leather uppers, most of us now walk around on synthetic soles.

Plastic fantastic

Both the upper and the sole of modern-day sneakers are often made completely from synthetic materials.

Shape Shifting

Just as fashionable dress has not always followed the natural contours of the human body, so shoes have not always followed the shape of the foot. Changing styles have taken shoes from long and narrow to wide and wedgy and back again, with pointed, rounded, or squared-off toes.

Making a point

Throughout medieval Europe turnshoes with pointed toes were popular. The fashion victims of the day stepped out in such long, narrow shoes that they had to tie the tips to garters around their knees.

Toeing the line

Early shoes were molded around the natural shape of the foot, but by the 12th century, European shoemakers were beginning to give shoes pointed toes. Nobles had the money to play with fashion, and by the end of the 14th century they were wearing narrow shoes with pointed tips that turned upward. In the English court, noblemen took this fashion to such extremes that they found it hard to walk, and laws were created to regulate shoe lengths!

During the 16th century, shoes became shorter and rounder, and a style called the duckbill came into fashion. Soon shapes began to change more frequently, and different styles came and went.

Royal Getup

Henry VIII of England was depicted wearing the latest fashion in this 1536 portrait, including duckbill shoes with cut-out patterns in the uppers. Padding was needed to maintain the shoes' wide shape.

Toe torture

Unlike the soft medieval turnshoes, the pointed shoes of the 1960s were stiff and unbending, and often gave their wearers corns, blisters, or even bunions. Strangely, they have rarely been out of fashion!

Sticking to the straight & narrow

In the 16th century, shoemakers were also producing footwear with absolutely straight sides and no distinction between the left and right shoe. It wasn't until the middle of the 19th century that different shoes were made for left and right feet.

Shoemaking machines were invented at about this time, making production quicker and cheaper. In turn, this meant that more and more people could afford to keep up with changing footwear fashions.

Hip to be Square

Fashions change so rapidly today that square toes can be in one season and out the next, as rounded or pointed toes take over again.

Bound feet

Tiny shoes like these were once worn by women in the Chinese Imperial Court. As young girls, their feet were bandaged tightly to keep them very small. The practice of foot-binding was banned in 1911.

Roman remains

The soles of Roman boots and work shoes were protected from hard surfaces by metal hobnails. The hobnail had a broad head and a short spike.

Sole Survivors

When the Romans expanded their empire and built paved roads throughout Europe, they needed sturdy boots for their marching soldiers. Short nails called hobnails were the answer. Hammered into the leather sole, hobnails protected it from wear and tear.

Old boots

In medieval times, boots were made from soft leather using the turnshoe method. Laces were leather, as well.

Soft-soled turnshoes

After the fall of their empire in 406 C.E., the Romans' shoemaking skills were forgotten. Hobnailed boots were replaced by the slipperlike turnshoe, made by sewing an upper and a sole together and then turning the shoe inside out. These shoes didn't wear well because even their soles had to be made from soft leather, so that the finished shoes would be flexible enough to turn.

Suede & crepe

The British Teddy boy styles of the 1950s included suede shoes with thick flat soles of crepe rubber.

Durable welted shoes

Toward the end of the Middle Ages, the turnshoe began to be replaced by the welted shoe, constructed with techniques still in use today. In a welted shoe, the upper is attached to the insole, then a strip called the welt is placed between the insole and the sole. Finally, the insole, welt, and sole are stitched together. Because welted shoes do not need to be turned inside out, their soles can be made from much sturdier materials than the soft leather used for turnshoes.

THESE BOOTS WERE MADE FOR WALKING

To help prevent the wearer from slipping, modern hiking boots have synthetic soles with heavily grooved treads.

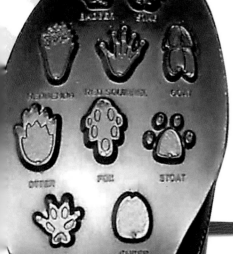

ANIMAL TRACKS

Unlike leather soles, synthetic ones can be molded into various shapes with patterned treads like these.

Shortages of leather during World War II (1939–1945) meant that shoe soles were sometimes made of cork or wood. The wedge shape of the sole made it stronger.

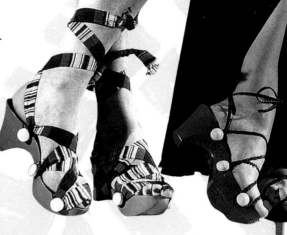

Modern manufacturing

Techniques for making soles changed very little until the 19th century. The big breakthrough came in 1858, when an American named Lyman R. Blake invented a machine for sewing the soles of shoes to the upper.

Although rubber-soled athletic shoes became popular in the 19th century, leather soles continued to be the first choice for other shoes until synthetic materials emerged in the 20th century. Today, the majority of shoe soles are made from synthetics, which are shaped in molds and then adhered to the upper.

WALKING ON AIR

Soles cushion our feet, as well as protect them. Contemporary designs include sneakers with air-filled soles.

Standing Tall

Thick-soled platform shoes were invented hundreds of years ago to raise the wearer's feet well above the mud and puddles of ancient streets. However, people have long had far more fashion-conscious reasons for wearing them. Platform soles make the wearer look taller and help him or her stand out in a crowd. In the past this also showed that the wearer was rich.

Shiny Chopines

The chopines worn by 16th-century Venetian ladies often had shaped platforms, which were covered in embroidered velvet and jewels.

Platformed Protectors

Early platforms were sometimes slipped on as overshoes, so that more precious shoes were lifted above muddy streets.

High society

No one made more of this height advantage than the court ladies of 16th-century Venice. Venetian platform shoes were known as chopines and the wearer could only stay upright with a servant holding on to each arm to support her. This impractical style didn't really catch on elsewhere in Europe, and it was soon replaced by a new trend: high heels.

Platform shoes didn't come back into fashion until the 20th century, when advances in shoe technology resulted in more practical designs.

Natural materials

Since their invention, the soles of platform shoes have been made from wood or, like this 1970s sandal, from cork.

Musical madness

Teeteringly high platform soles put the finishing touch on the outrageous stage costumes worn by the Glam rockers of the 1970s.

See-through stompers

Wacky 1970s designs included platform shoes with transparent heels.

Stepping out in style

Shoe designers such as Italian Salvatore Ferragamo (1898–1960) came up with a range of innovative styles in the 1930s, including wedged platform shoes, which were widely copied. Platforms remained in fashion until 1947, when the New Look brought more elegant heels back into vogue.

The remainder of the century saw two further revivals of the platform shoe. The first was led by the Glam rock stars of the 1970s. The second came in the 1990s, when the ultra-high designs included the 7-in (20-cm) platform shoe that model Naomi Campbell tripped on during a 1994 fashion show.

Dedicated followers of fashion

Platform shoes and boots were seen on the streets as well as on the stage in the 1970s. As in 16th-century Venice, wearers sometimes needed a shoulder to lean on to help them stay upright.

Well-Heeled

No one knows exactly when or why the heel was invented. Shoes that were raised above the ground were worn in ancient times, but these shoes were probably a form of platform. Early platform shoes were notoriously difficult to get around on, and at some stage someone found that by making the heel higher than the sole you obtained height while still being able to keep your balance.

Tall story?

One theory is that the heel was invented for horseback riding, to stop the rider's foot from slipping out of the stirrup.

Fashionable French queen

We do know, however, that heeled shoes were worn in the French court during the 16th century. The French queen, Catherine de' Medici (1519–1589), made the style popular after buying heeled shoes from an Italian shoemaker. During the next 100 years the fashion spread throughout the courts of Europe, with heels growing higher and being worn by noblemen and noblewomen alike.

Courting compliments

These 17th-century silk shoes are embroidered with silver thread. The splayed heel is known as a Louis heel.

High-heeled shoes are completely unsuitable for manual labor, and for centuries they were only worn by the nobility. Made of richly decorated leather, satin, or velvet, the shoes were also extremely costly. It wasn't until the 18th century that a heeled shoe was adopted by the monied middle classes. Even then, their shoes had lower heels than those worn by court nobles.

Victorian high fashion

High-heeled shoes were a must for fashionable ladies in the late 19th century, and replaced the flat shoes worn since the early 1800s.

TWENTIES GLAMOUR

In the 1920s, skirts rose to knee length and women's shoes became very visible. The shaped heels and beautiful decoration of these evening shoes are typical of the period.

Reaching new heights

A tall, narrow heel containing a thin steel core was invented in Italy in the early 1950s. It is known as the stiletto. Its strength lay in its steel core, and two shoe designers are famous for developing its potential: Salvatore Ferragamo and French designer Roger Vivier (1913–1998). Vivier worked with another French designer, Christian Dior (1905–1957), creating shoes to go with Dior's postwar collections. Ferragamo was shoemaker to many Hollywood stars, including Marilyn Monroe. His heels may be responsible for her famous walk.

PERENNIAL FAVORITE

Stiletto heels are popular, despite doctors' warnings that they can result in injuries and foot damage. The lower version (above) is a safer option.

WELL-HEELED CLIENTS

Cuban-heeled boots for men took off in the 1960s after Roger Vivier made them for the Beatles. Vivier's other clients included Queen Elizabeth II, for whom he designed the shoes she wore at her 1953 coronation.

The Ties That Bind

All sorts of shoe fastenings have been invented over the years. The early Egyptians used a thong-style strap held between the toes, while in India people gripped a knob on the shoe sole in much the same way. Roman shoes were tied on with leather laces, as were North American moccasins and the turnshoes of medieval Europe.

Romance with the rose

The welted shoe had a far sturdier construction than the turnshoe, and its introduction at the end of the Middle Ages opened up creative possibilities for ensuring that shoes stayed on the feet. Large fabric rosette fastners were a popular shoe decoration at European courts during the first part of the 17th century. Often they were embroidered with gold or silver thread and small jewels to make them sparkle.

Ankle boot

This child's turnshoe from the late 14th century has leather laces to hold it safely around the ankle. The laces are threaded through holes punched into the soft leather.

Ribbons and bows

By the end of the 17th century it had become fashionable for court nobles to tie their shoes with extravagant bows made from broad ribbons. Ordinary people used narrower ribbons and made smaller bows.

One, two, buckle my shoe

Metal buckles became common during the 18th century, while in the 19th century tightly laced or buttoned boots were popular. Elastic-sided boots date back to the 1830s. Easier to pull on or off than buttoned or laced footwear, elasticized boots had been widely adopted by the early 1900s. Buttons and laces didn't vanish, though—they went in and out of fashion throughout the 20th century.

BEAUTIFUL BUCKLES

Big, plain shoe buckles like these were all the rage at the end of the 18th century. At other times, more decorative buckles were preferred.

All zipped up

The forerunner of the modern zipper was the slide fastener patented by Whitcomb L. Judson in 1893 in the United States. The word "zipper" comes from the trade name for the rubber boots with slide fasteners that were introduced by the B.F. Goodrich Company in 1923. It wasn't until after World War II that zippers became widely available outside of the United States.

STYLISH SPATS

Spats, first popular in the 1890s–1900s, were cloth shoe-coverings. They experienced a small revival in the 1980s.

ZIPPY SHOES

Although today a familiar fastening for boots and shoes, the zipper didn't come into general use until the second half of the 20th century.

STRETCHY FASTENINGS

The buttons on these Victorian boots are just for decoration. The boots' elastic sides made pulling them on and off easy and quick.

STICKY STRIPS

Velcro was introduced as a shoe fastening in the late 20th century. Swiss engineer Georges de Mestral came up with the idea in the 1940s when pulling plant burs from his pants' legs.

Slip on a Sandal

The sandal is one of the oldest kinds of shoe, with an open, airy structure that makes it ideal for hot weather. The ancient Egyptians made simple thong-style sandals from papyrus reeds, but later they also used palm fronds or leather. Wall paintings show that the nobility had jewels woven into their sandals for special occasions.

Palm perfection

Woven from palm fronds, this Egyptian sandal was the forerunner of the plastic flip-flop worn worldwide today.

Air conditioning

The open top and latticework sides of this Roman sandal allowed air to circulate around the foot. Roman sandals were designed to support the foot and could reach well above the ankle.

Design developments

The ancient Greeks wore a simple leather sole strapped to the foot with ties that sometimes continued a short way up the leg. The Romans reworked the basic design, making a more complex sandal from a lattice of woven leather.

In the ancient world, slaves often went barefoot. Sandals were a sign of wealth. It was a different story in the cold climate of northern Europe. During the Middle Ages, sandals were worn by monks and priests and were regarded as a sign of their piety and frugal lifestyles.

Eastern elegance

Sandals have been worn in Japan for centuries. The wooden sandals worn by the lady on the right are called getas and, along with the kimono, are part of Japan's traditional costume.

SHOCK ABSORBERS

Even on cool days, a long-distance walk can be sweaty work. The latest hiking sandals cushion the sole while letting the rest of the foot breathe.

Style statements

By the 1930s, improvements in shoe technology had made a strappy, high-heeled sandal possible, and this style became a hot fashion item. The sandals displayed the neat toe seam of the latest nylon stockings, along with the newly respectable painted toenails.

The hippie movement of the 1960s ushered in a craze for flat leather sandals, including Indian styles that were held on to the foot by a loop around the big toe. A decade later, orthopedic shoes went mainstream, as Birkenstocks and wooden-soled Dr. Scholl's sandals became fashionable. The final decade of the 20th century saw the development of the ultracomfortable, high-tech hiking sandal.

OLD FAVORITES

Plastic flip-flops were given a fashion makeover in 2000–2001. Soles were brightly colored and patterned. The thong was transparent, beaded, or decorated with flowers.

HAPPY HIPPIES

Cheap leather sandals were an essential part of the colorful, loose-fitting garb of the 1960s.

Athlete's Feet

Special shoes for sports are a fairly recent development in the history of footwear. They emerged in the 19th century, prompted by a new understanding of the value of exercise in building and maintaining physical health.

Playing the field

In Great Britain, for example, exercise periods were built into the schedules of all 19th century schools. Heavy boots, often with steel toecaps and metal-studded soles, were worn for sports such as soccer and rugby.

The rubber-soled canvas sneaker, known as the plimsoll in Britain, was patented in 1876. Because it was relatively inexpensive, it allowed more people to participate in sports, both in school and out.

Meanwhile, the popularity of the bicycle led to boots with broad heels for gripping the pedals.

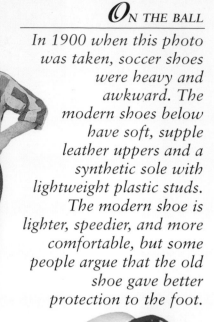

On the ball

In 1900 when this photo was taken, soccer shoes were heavy and awkward. The modern shoes below have soft, supple leather uppers and a synthetic sole with lightweight plastic studs. The modern shoe is lighter, speedier, and more comfortable, but some people argue that the old shoe gave better protection to the foot.

Get your skates on

Invented in the 18th century, roller skating soon became a fashionable hobby. The skates above date from the 1880s, when they were strapped to ordinary shoes. Contemporary in-line skates (right) come attached to special boots that provide strong ankle support. In-line skating didn't take off until the 1980s, although enthusiasts began developing the sport in the early 20th century.

*G*OLF SHOES

Golf shoes, like all sports shoes, are the subject of ongoing research and redesign. Modeled on men's brogues, today's golf shoes are sturdy lace-ups with studded soles for traction. They are often two-tone in color.

*H*OLD TIGHT

To prevent feet from slipping out of rock crevices, modern climbing shoes have very high-grip rubber soles.

*S*hock-resistant shoes

The forerunner of the modern athletic shoe was the canvas All Star basketball shoe. It was introduced in 1919 by American Converse. A major technological breakthrough came in 1971, when Bill Bowerman of the Nike company invented the high-traction sole by shaping rubber in his wife's waffle iron.

This was rapidly followed by the air sole, in which air-filled pockets cushion the impact as the foot pounds against the ground.

The fitness boom of the past 30 years has seen an explosion in the design and manufacture of athletic shoes, with versions specially engineered for the specific demands of individual sports, from running to rock climbing.

*W*HAT'S IN A NAME?

In the 1980s, a passion for sports shoes went hand-in-hand with the boom in extreme sports such as BMX and skateboarding. The coolest athletes didn't wear any old sneakers—brand names were everything.

Shoes as Art

Although their function is to protect the feet, shoes can also be beautiful, highly decorative, and even, like the 16th-century Venetian chopines, extremely impractical. Advances in shoe manufacturing during the 20th century, along with a growing choice of materials, resulted in innovative original designs that are more like works of art than everyday footwear.

Monkeying Around

In the 1930s, Italian-born fashion designer Elsa Schiaparelli (1890–1973) became famous for her witty and often shocking designs. Made in about 1937, these monkey-fur boots are typical of her surreal sense of humor.

Influenced by artists

Neither art nor design happens in a vacuum, and contemporary clothing and shoe designers are often inspired by the work of painters and sculptors. Some designers start their training in art colleges—Roger Vivier, for instance, originally studied to be a sculptor. In addition to Roger Vivier and Salvatore Ferragamo, leading shoe designers of the 20th century have included the Spanish designer Manolo Blahnik (1940–) (whose shoes were made famous by the TV show "Sex and the City") and British designers Patrick Cox (1963–) and Vivienne Westwood (1941–).

Fascinated by fish

André Perugia created this bizarre fish shoe, complete with tail fins, scales, and eyes, in 1931, as a tribute to the still-life paintings of the artist Georges Braque (1882–1963).

SEEING IS BELIEVING?

A painting by the Belgian surrealist René Magritte (1898–1937), in which clothes and shoes take on the shape of the wearer's body, inspired the extraordinary shoes below. They were created during the 1980s for the French couturier Pierre Cardin (1922–).

MONDRIAN ON THE MOVE

The abstract, grid-like paintings of Dutch-born artist Piet Mondrian (1872–1944) have influenced everything from fabrics to footwear. These shoes were created in 1950 by the French designer Charles Jourdan (1883–1976).

SCULPTURAL CURVES

Designers often seem to regard shoes as sculpture for the feet, creating playful variations on standard sole and heel shapes.

Men in Boots

Boots first became high-fashion footwear in the 17th century, when the Cavaliers who supported King Charles I of England (1600–1649) began wearing riding boots inside. Cavalier boots, as they became known, were funnel shaped, with a deep cuff at the knee, low heels, and spurs.

Birth of the Wellington

In the late 18th century, a straight-sided, black riding boot with a contrasting brown top was popularized by the English dandy and fashion leader Beau Brummell (1778–1840). This evolved into the Wellington boot. Made of plain black leather in those days, it was named in honor of the Duke of Wellington (1769–1852), who was hailed as a hero after his 1815 victory over the French leader Napoleon (1769–1821) at the Battle of Waterloo.

ROMANTIC ROYALISTS

The Cavaliers were romantic and flamboyant dressers. Their boots were sometimes worn with ornamental spurs (above left and right), or with lace-topped stockings (above center).

HERO IN BOOTS

In Britain, the Duke of Wellington (above) was immortalized by the boots named in his honor. Today's Wellingtons are made from rubber or plastic, and come in a range of colors.

QUICK MARCH

A pair of sturdy boots has been an important part of the well-equipped soldier's kit since Roman times.

COWBOY GEAR

Cowboy boots have been fashionable since the late 1960s. The pointed toe, curved top, and tapered heel are their most distinctive features.

DOCTOR KNOWS BEST

Originally designed as work boots, Dr. Martens have been worn by groups as diverse as hippies and skinheads. Today they are available in many colors and a wide range of heights.

A boom in boots

In the 1960s the prosperity that followed World War II combined with a baby boom to produce large numbers of affluent teenagers. The new shoe styles that catered to this market included the suede desert boot and the Cuban-heeled Beatles boot.

The most enduring boot was the Dr. (or Doc) Martens. The original boot was black with yellow stitching, and the first pair rolled off the production line on April 1, 1960. The Doc Marten became standard issue for mail carriers, police officers, and many factory workers, before being adopted by skinheads, punk rockers, and mainstream teenagers.

Women's Boots

IN THE PAST, BOOTS WERE WORN only by women who lived in cold climates. The traditional dress of the Inuit peoples of Alaska, northern Canada, and Greenland, for instance, has always included animal-skin boots for both men and women. In warmer climates, boots were mainly for men, except for women's leather horseback riding boots.

Victorian values

In the early 19th century, the tightly laced or buttoned ankle boot became fashionable for women. By the century's end, heeled ankle boots or the newer calf height footwear in waterproof leather or cloth were an integral part of the stylish women's wardrobe.

During the first half of the 20th century, it became fashionable to display a well-shaped ankle in the new nylon stockings, so boots returned to being a utilitarian item reserved for bad weather.

VICTORIAN BOOTS

In the 19th century, the calf height boots worn during the day allowed Victorian women to wear their skirt hemlines slightly higher, while still modestly covering their ankles.

WOMEN IN WHITE

In the 1960s designer André Courrèges paired white boots with his miniskirts. The boots came in plastic or leather, and went as high as the calf, knee, or thigh.

RUNAWAY SUCCESS

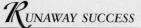

Skintight leather boots like these reached cult status after they were worn by actress Diana Rigg in the 1960s TV series The Avengers. Snugly fitting boots would have been impossible without the invention of the zipper.

YETI BOOTS

Shaped like the moon boots of the 1970s, but hairier, the Yeti boot had a moment of fame when worn by Samantha Mumba at a London awards ceremony in 2001.

26

Re-booting

The women's fashion boot resurfaced in the 1960s, when French fashion designer André Courrèges (1923–) complemented his sharply angular miniskirts with flat white boots. When hemlines dropped again in the 1970s, midiskirts were worn over skintight platform boots, but it wasn't until the 1980s and 1990s that boot styles really began to multiply.

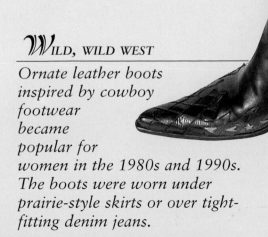

Beauty and the Boot

Thigh-high, stiletto-heeled boots often enjoy a revival when worn by a superstar, like Kylie Minogue shown here in 2002.

Wild, Wild West

Ornate leather boots inspired by cowboy footwear became popular for women in the 1980s and 1990s. The boots were worn under prairie-style skirts or over tight-fitting denim jeans.

Sturdy Fashion

Work boots, for women as well as men, have been in and out of fashion from the 1960s until today.

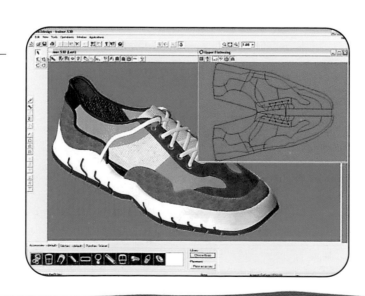

Technology of the Shoe

Up until the mid-19th century all shoes were made by hand, with shoemakers using virtually the same tools that were around in ancient Egyptian times. The mechanization of shoemaking was made possible by the first practical sewing machine, patented by American inventor Elias Howe (1819–1867) in 1846.

Early automation

Two Americans adapted Howe's invention for use in shoemaking. In 1858 Lyman R. Blake patented a machine for sewing the soles of shoes to uppers. His equipment was improved by Gordon McKay (1821–1903). The next key invention was the shoe-lasting machine, patented in 1883 by Jan Ernst Matzeliger (1852–1889). The last is a foot-shaped form over which the upper is shaped and attached to the sole. By the century's end, these and other new machines had led to the mass production of footwear in factories, and a lowering of costs.

UPPER

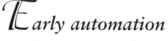

INSERT

MIDSOLE

OUTSOLE

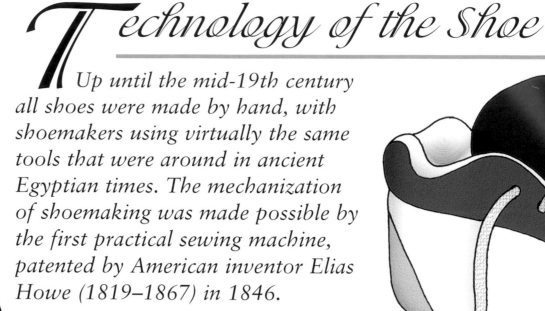

The upper, of ever-lighter material, holds the sole onto the foot. The insert is shaped to the foot arch, cushions the foot, and helps keep it cool and dry. The crucial midsole gives the most cushioning and is the subject of constant design innovation. The outsole provides grip and, importantly, protects the midsole.

Modern manufacture

These days shoe manufacturing involves dozens of stages, beginning with the design. Once this has been approved, patterns are made for each part in each size of the shoe. The upper parts are cut out and then stitched or glued together. Next the upper is pulled over the last in a lasting machine and stitched or glued to the insole, midsole, and outsole. Finally, a heel is sometimes attached and a removable insert fitted.

Today computers are involved in many of these stages. Shoes may be designed on a computer, for instance, and manufacturing equipment is often computer-controlled. Some shoes even have computers built into them. Patented in 1999, for instance, the Raven shoe has a battery-powered microchip that responds to the wearer's need for foot cushioning by inflating or deflating a tiny air bladder in the sole!

Even the best-designed shoes will harm feet if they don't fit properly. Modern measuring machines use electronic sensors to make an exact map of the foot and judge the correct shoe size.

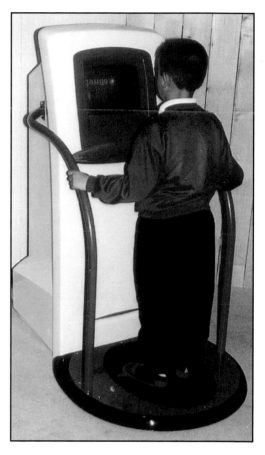

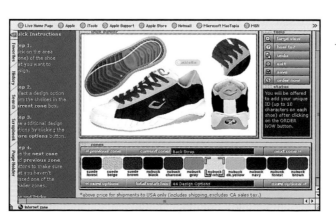

Do-it-yourself design

Buying footwear via the Internet is old news these days. The new news is that there are websites where you can customize your shoes before they are manufactured, choosing a style and specifying your own materials and colors.

Timeline

Prehistory
In cold regions, the first shoes were animal skins wrapped around the feet or sewn into foot bags.

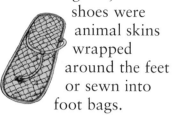

The ancient world
The ancient Egyptians made papyrus sandals as early as 3700 B.C.E. By the 1st century C.E, the Romans were making shoes with uppers, insoles, and tough, hobnailed soles. Their footwear was far more complex than anything else worn at the time, but after the fall of their empire in the 5th century C.E., the Romans' shoemaking skills were forgotten.

The Middle Ages
In Europe, in the Middle Ages (500-1500 C.E.), people wore a simple shoe known as the turnshoe. By the 14th century, turnshoes were long and narrow with pointed toes. In the following century, this style gave way to the wide-toed duckbill shoe. By the end of the Middle Ages, the turnshoe was being replaced by the sturdier welted shoe.

16th century
In Venice women adopted an extreme style called the chopine which had very high platform soles. Elsewhere, heels were attached to the soles of riding boots, to help keep the foot in the stirrup. Court nobles wore high-heeled shoes to exaggerate their height and social status. Shoemakers found heeled shoes more difficult to make. To overcome this, they made shoes with straight sides—there was no distinction between the right and the left foot.

17th century
In the French court, shoes with very high heels were worn by both men and women. Made of wood, the heels were covered with the same fine cloth as the shoe. Cavalier boots were fashionable footwear for the supporters of King Charles I of England (1600–1649). The boots were funnel shaped and knee length, with deep, cuffed tops. During the reign of King Charles II (1630–1685), heeled shoes became fashionable again for men, this time decorated with a large, soft bow.

18th century
Stylish men either wore shoes with large buckles, or long, straight, black riding boots. For most of the century, women wore heeled shoes, but when the high-waisted gown came in at the end of the century, heeled shoes were replaced by flat slippers.

19th century
Women's shoes continued to be flat until the second half of the century. For men, boots started to be reserved for riding and other outdoor pursuits. In the 1830s, elastic-sided boots were introduced and became immediately popular for day wear. The canvas, rubber-soled sports shoe known as the sneaker was first made in the 1870s. From the middle of the century onward, shoemaking was revolutionized by the invention of special machinery. By the century's end, different shoes for the left and right feet were being made.

20th century & beyond
A wide range of styles were available for men by the early 1900s, and in the 1920s, brogues became popular. Women's styles began to vary, as skirt lengths rose and shoes became more visible. The knee-length flapper dress of the 1920s was worn with multicolored shoes with decorated heels. The stiletto heel was invented in the mid-1950s and became an enduring style. The 1960s also saw the launch of the Dr. Martens boot. The platform shoe came back into fashion in the 1970s, and in the 1980s, advances in synthetic materials and manufacturing led to the creation of the high-tech sneaker. By the beginning of the 21st century, footwear fashions were changing every season, with designers borrowing from the past and looking to the future.

Glossary

brogue laced man's shoe with punched decoration on the upper. It became fashionable in the 1920s.

chopine extremely high platform shoe, worn in the 16th century by Venetian ladies

cuban heel medium-height heel with a slightly tapered back. It first appeared in the late 1900s.

desert boot suede ankle-boot with a crepe sole, originally developed for soldiers taking part in desert campaigns during World War II

duckbill style of turnshoe with an extremely wide toe, popular in the 15th century

insole lining placed inside a shoe for warmth or comfort

last foot-shaped form on which the upper is shaped and then attached to the sole

Louis heel medium-height heel, tapered on all sides and flared at the base

moccasin slipperlike leather shoe, often decorated with beading, originally worn by Native Americans

platform shoe with a very thick sole

sole underside of a shoe, without the heel

stiletto tall, narrow-heeled shoe containing a thin steel core for sturdiness

tread part of a shoe sole that touches the ground, often grooved or knobbed to provide grip

turnshoe shoe named for its method of construction—the upper and sole were stitched together, then the shoe was turned inside out. The turnshoe was worn in Europe throughout the Middle Ages, until replaced by the welted shoe.

upper topmost part of a shoe

Wellington boot (Wellingtons) waterproof boot, today made from rubber or plastic

welted shoe form of shoe construction introduced toward the end of the Middle Ages and still used today. The welt is a strip placed between the insole and sole, and then stitched to them.

Index